AMERICA IN WORDS AND SONG

The Declaration of Independence

The Story Behind Our Founding Document

Kerry A. Graves

CHELSEA
CLUBHOUSE

An Imprint of Chelsea House Publishers
A Haights Cross Communications Company
Philadelphia

Chelsea Clubhouse books are published by
Chelsea House Publishers, a subsidiary of
Haights Cross Communications Company.

A Haights Cross Communications ◀ Company

The Chelsea House World Wide Web address is
www.chelseahouse.com

Printed and bound in the United States of America.

9 8 7 6 5 4 3 2 1

Library of Congress Cataloging-in-Publication Data
Graves, Kerry A.
  The Declaration of Independence : the story behind America's
founding document / by Kerry A. Graves.
    p. cm. — (America in words and song)
Summary: Focuses on the framing of the Declaration of
Independence and the meaning of the document, describing the
circumstances leading to the Revolutionary War and some of the
challenges faced by the men who wrote the document.
Includes bibliographical references and index.
  ISBN 0-7910-7334-3
1. United States. Declaration of Independence—Juvenile literature.
2. United States—Politics and government—To 1775—Juvenile
literature. 3. United States—Politics and government—
1775–1783—Juvenile literature. [1. United States. Declaration of
Independence. 2. United States—Politics and government—To
1775. 3. United States—Politics and government—1775–1783.]
I. Title. II. Series.
E221.G87 2004
973.3'13—dc21   2003004037

Selected Sources

Becker, Carl L. *The Declaration of Independence: A Study in the
History of Political Ideas*. Birmingham, Ala.: Palladium Press,
2002 [first published 1922].

Hakim, Joy. *From Colonies to Country. A History of US*. Book
Three. New York: Oxford University Press, 1999.

Hawke, David Freeman. *A Transaction of Free Men: The Birth
and Course of the Declaration of Independence*. New York:
DaCapo Press, 1989 [first published 1964].

Maier, Pauline. *American Scripture: Making the Declaration of
Independence*. New York: Knopf, 1997.

National Archives and Records Administration: The Charters
of Freedom.
www.archives.gov/exhibit_hall/charters_of_freedom/
charters_of_freedom.html

Editorial Credits

Colleen Sexton, editor; Takeshi Takahashi, designer;
Keith Trego, layout; Mary Englar, photo researcher

Photo Credits

Library of Congress: cover (Second Continental Congress),
23; © Joseph Sohm/CORBIS: cover (document), 19, 25
(bottom); © Bettmann/CORBIS: title page, 10, 11, 14, 15, 18
(bottom); Hulton/Archive by Getty Images: 4, 6, 8, 13; Stock
Montage, Inc.: 7, 16; North Wind Picture Archives: 9, 12, 17, 18
(top), 22; © Peter Turnley/CORBIS: 24; © Underwood &
Underwood/CORBIS: 25 (top); AP/Wide World: 26, 27, 30

Table of Contents

Introduction

On a May day in 1607, three English ships reached the eastern coast of America, the land Europeans called the New World. About 100 men and boys were aboard with plans to establish an English settlement. They chose a site near the James River, in what is now Virginia, and built a triangular fort surrounding small shelters. Survival was difficult, but Jamestown endured and became the first permanent English settlement in America.

England, like other European countries, was eager to claim America's riches. As more English settlers established towns and farmed the land, they were expected to send crops and natural resources—such as lumber, furs, and fish—back to their homeland. These **exports** brought great wealth to England. In 1707 Scotland joined England and they became Great Britain. In turn, **colonists** depended on Britain for manufactured items. British trading ships brought furniture, tools, cookware, cloth, and other necessities to the colonies. Some British ships also brought African slaves, who were sold as property and forced to work without pay.

At first, the Jamestown settlers traded with American Indians, who had lived in North America for thousands of years. But as the colonists took more and more Indian land, the two groups began attacking one another.

More settlers arrived. Most were British, but other Europeans came, too. They had heard stories about plentiful land and religious freedom in America. In all, these **immigrants** established 13 colonies along America's eastern coast.

A sense of unity grew among the colonists. As they struggled together to build a new life in a new land, the colonists developed an independent spirit. They thought for themselves and believed anything could be achieved through hard work. Americans became richer as trade thrived between the colonies and Britain. The colonists were loyal to and supported Britain's king. In the 1760s, however, Britain slowly started to tighten its control over the 13 colonies. The freedoms the colonists enjoyed were being threatened.

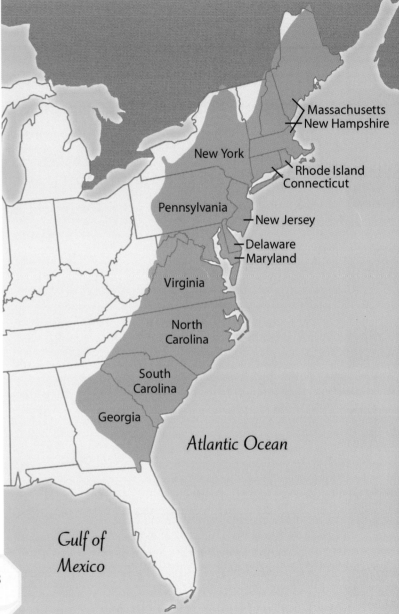

Massachusetts
New Hampshire
New York
Rhode Island
Connecticut
Pennsylvania
New Jersey
Delaware
Maryland
Virginia
North Carolina
South Carolina
Georgia
Atlantic Ocean
Gulf of Mexico

By the 1730s, Britain had 13 colonies in North America.

A Call for War

Britain's policies in the colonies began to change after the French and Indian War (1754–1763). Colonists had fought alongside British soldiers in this struggle against France for control of North America. The war ended with a British victory, and the country gained large areas of land to the north and west of the 13 colonies. But Britain was left with a huge war debt and needed even more money to support British troops sent to guard the newly won territories. The British government decided the colonists should help pay these costs through extra taxes.

General William Johnson of New York and his 1,500 colonial troops defeated French forces in the Battle of Lake George. This battle was one of many fought in America, Canada, and Europe during the French and Indian War.

The Stamp Act, passed in 1765, required colonists to buy stamps such as the ones shown here and put them on certain printed items.

When the British **Parliament** started passing new tax laws, the colonists protested. Not only had the colonists fought side by side with the British, but they had also helped fund the war effort with their own money. The colonists believed they had the right to approve taxes through elected representatives just as other British citizens did. But the colonists did not have representatives in the British Parliament. Therefore, the colonists concluded, Parliament should not tax them. The colonists called it "taxation without representation" and saw it as **tyranny**, or cruel and unjust rule.

But Parliament went ahead with its plans. In 1765, Britain passed the Stamp Act, which declared that colonists had to buy stamps to put on all printed items sold or handed out in the colonies. The Stamp Act taxed everything from legal documents to newspapers to playing cards. In 1767, the Townshend Acts added new taxes on **imported** lead, glass, paper, paint, and tea.

These new tax laws angered the colonists and spurred them to action. There were riots. Mobs of colonists forced many stamp tax collectors to quit their jobs. Colonists also refused to buy British products. This **boycott** meant that Britain made almost no money at all by taxing goods they sent to America. Soon Parliament threw out all the taxes except the one on tea. But even that small tax led frustrated colonists in Massachusetts to dump British tea into Boston Harbor in 1773. In response to this "Boston Tea Party," the British government closed Boston Harbor and put Massachusetts under military control in 1774. Many colonists called the harsh new laws against Massachusetts the Intolerable Acts.

Colonists believed Parliament had no right to pass the Stamp Act. To protest, they refused to buy stamps and rioted in the streets.

On the night of December 16, 1773, a crowd gathered at Griffin's Wharf in Boston Harbor. Three ships filled with cases of British tea had been docked at the wharf for almost three weeks. But the port of Boston wouldn't allow the ships to be unloaded. People throughout the 13 colonies were opposed to a British tax and would not buy the tea. The colonists tried to make the ships return to Britain with the tea still on board. But British officials refused to give permission for the "tea ships" to leave Boston Harbor. Now the colonists were taking the matter into their own hands.

With the crowd's approval, about 150 men boarded the ships. They had disguised themselves as Mohawk Indians, smearing their faces with coal dust and red paint. Some wrapped blankets around their shoulders. Some carried hatchets. The colonists worked through the night, breaking open 342 chests of valuable tea stored in the ships' holds. By dawn, the men had dumped all of the tea overboard.

This event came to be known as the Boston Tea Party, an action that angered Britain's King George III. He had Parliament pass laws that closed Boston Harbor and put the entire colony of Massachusetts under military control. King George thought it would serve as an example to the other colonies. Instead, it unified the colonies and pushed them toward war.

Colonists dressed as Mohawk Indians dumped tea from three British ships into Boston Harbor. This event became known as the Boston Tea Party.

Patrick Henry of Virginia addressed the First Continental Congress in 1774, a meeting of 56 colonial representatives. The group discussed how to make Britain respect the colonists' rights.

Political leaders from each American colony had been writing to each other for many years. In 1774, they planned a meeting in Philadelphia to discuss the problems with Britain. Every colony except Georgia sent **delegates** to the meeting, called the First Continental Congress. The men met for seven weeks, beginning on September 5. At the end of the session, the delegates advised the colonists to stop trading with Britain and to form local fighting groups called **militias**. They also sent a respectful letter of complaint to Britain's King George III, hoping Britain would treat its citizens in the American colonies better. The representatives agreed to meet again in May 1775 if the situation with Britain didn't improve.

Tensions grew between the colonists and British soldiers stationed in America. In Massachusetts, the militia had stored cannons and gunpowder in the town of Concord. When spies told British soldiers about the storehouse, the British decided to capture the weapons. But the colonists had spies of their own who learned of the British plan. On the night of April 18, 1775, Paul Revere, William Dawes, and Dr. Samuel Prescott all rode on horseback to warn the colonists that the British soldiers were coming. The militia fought these "redcoats" at the towns of Lexington and Concord. No one knows who fired the first shot, but writer Ralph Waldo Emerson later called it "the shot heard round the world." The Revolutionary War had begun.

The Revolutionary War began on April 19, 1775, when colonists and British soldiers exchanged fire at the towns of Lexington and Concord in Massachusetts.

11

The Second Continental Congress

As planned, the Second Continental Congress met at the State House in Philadelphia on May 10, 1775. The delegates still hoped to settle the colonists' disagreement with Britain, but first they had to keep the British Army from taking over. In June, the Congress took control of the militia that had gathered in Massachusetts. The delegates selected George Washington to command this new Continental Army.

While the delegates met, war continued. In May, American troops captured Fort Ticonderoga and another fort at nearby Crown Point. Both forts were on an important river route between Canada and New York City. In Massachusetts, the colonial militia fought for control of hills that overlooked Boston. From there, they would be able to aim their guns at the British Army stationed in the city. The British attacked, and the Americans battled back until they ran out of **ammunition**. Although the British Army won this fight, called the Battle of Bunker Hill, more than 1,000 of its soldiers died. The American forces lost only a few men.

British soldiers—called "redcoats" for their red uniforms—march uphill to meet American troops in the Battle of Bunker Hill, the bloodiest fight of the Revolutionary War.

The Continental Congress met throughout 1775, still working to end the feud with Britain. In July, the delegates prepared another letter to King George III. This **petition** asked the king to stop his government's mistreatment of the colonies. It stated that the colonists were still loyal to their king and only wanted their rights to be respected. The letter became known as the "Olive Branch Petition," because a branch of an olive tree is a symbol of peace. But King George did not answer the petition. Instead, he said the Americans were rebels who wanted to break away from Britain and form an independent country. Then he hired German soldiers to help his redcoats defeat the colonists.

"Is life so dear, or peace so sweet, as to be purchased at the price of chains and slavery? Forbid it, Almighty God! I know not what course others may take; but as for me, give me liberty, or give me death!"
—Patrick Henry, member of the Virginia House of Burgesses, March 23, 1775

In July 1775, colonists sent the Olive Branch Petition to King George III. This photograph shows the first page of that letter.

The delegates to the Second Continental Congress debated independence from Britain at the State House in Philadelphia. Today, this historic landmark is known as Independence Hall.

News of the king's actions reached the colonies in early 1776. Although they were hesitant to do so, the delegates decided the colonies must separate from Britain. On June 7, Richard Henry Lee, a delegate from Virginia, asked the Congress to approve an important **resolution**:

> "That these United Colonies are, and of Right ought to be, Free and Independent States; that they are Absolved from all Allegiance to the British Crown, and that all political connection between them and the State of Great Britain, is and ought to be, totally dissolved."

Congress discussed Lee's resolution behind closed doors. Although the delegates agreed it was time for the colonists to declare their independence, some wanted to wait. Before taking that step, these delegates said, they needed the support and permission of their colonies. The Congress decided to put off a vote on the resolution until early July.

Thomas Paine was born in England and moved to the American colonies in 1774. He worked as a writer in Philadelphia. A strong supporter of American independence, Paine wrote a short pamphlet about the difficulties between the colonies and Britain. He called it *Common Sense*.

Paine gave clear, sensible reasons why the colonies should be independent. He argued that a **monarchy**, where a king or queen ruled over everyone, was an unjust form of government. In fact, he opposed all forms of rule that allowed people to **inherit** their offices. Paine thought the only good form of government was a republic, in which the people choose all their rulers. He also pointed out that it was silly for an island thousands of miles away to try to rule the whole North American continent.

Published in January 1776, the pamphlet sold more than 500,000 copies within a few months. Paine convinced many colonists, including members of the Continental Congress, that they should be free of Britain.

In his 1776 pamphlet, *Common Sense*, Thomas Paine argued for independence.

COMMON SENSE:

ADDRESSED TO THE

INHABITANTS

OF

AMERICA.

On the following interesting

SUBJECTS.

I. Of the Origin and Design of Government in general, with concise Remarks on the English Constitution.

II. Of Monarchy and Hereditary Succession.

III. Thoughts on the present State of American Affairs.

IV. Of the present Ability of America, with some miscellaneous Reflections.

Written by an ENGLISHMAN.

By Thomas Paine

Man knows no Master save creating HEAVEN,
Or those whom choice and common good ordain.
THOMSON.

PHILADELPHIA, Printed
And Sold by R. BELL, in Third-Street, 1776.

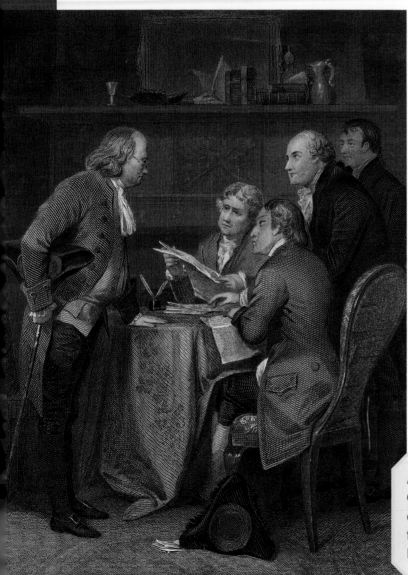

While waiting for a final vote on separation from Britain, the Congress appointed five delegates to write an official statement explaining why the colonies should be independent. A tall, quiet delegate from Virginia named Thomas Jefferson led this "Committee of Five," as they came to be known. Other members were Roger Sherman of Connecticut and Robert R. Livingston of New York. The Congress also selected John Adams of Massachusetts, a talkative delegate who strongly favored independence. The famous inventor and politician Benjamin Franklin of Pennsylvania also served on the committee.

A small group of delegates, known as the Committee of Five, drafted a document to explain why the colonies wanted to separate from Britain. This document became the Declaration of Independence.

The group first worked together to create an outline for the Declaration of Independence. The members then appointed Thomas Jefferson of Virginia to write a draft. He was well respected for his sharp mind and clear writing style. From June 11 to June 28, Jefferson labored over the draft. Finally, he made a copy of his original draft, and the Committee of Five made some revisions before sending it to the whole Congress on June 28.

On July 2, the delegates passed Lee's resolution and started to study the committee's document. For two days, the delegates changed words, cut out parts of the text, and rewrote or rearranged some sections of the document. They left Jefferson's opening paragraphs nearly as they were. Most of their efforts focused on revising the ending, a section on which Jefferson probably had little time to work.

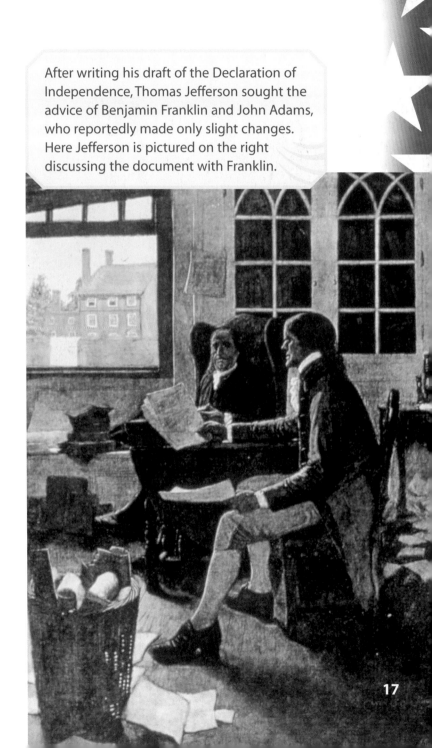

After writing his draft of the Declaration of Independence, Thomas Jefferson sought the advice of Benjamin Franklin and John Adams, who reportedly made only slight changes. Here Jefferson is pictured on the right discussing the document with Franklin.

News of the Declaration of Independence spread throughout the new 13 states. In Philadelphia, crowds cheered at a reading of the document (right). New Yorkers celebrated by tearing down a statue of King George III (below).

By late afternoon on July 4, the Declaration of Independence was finished. John Hancock, the president of the Congress, put his large signature at the bottom of the document. The Congress then had copies of the Declaration printed as a **broadside** and sent to what were now being called the 13 states. Copies also went to the commanders of the Continental Army to be read to their soldiers. Crowds gathered to hear the Declaration of Independence read out loud. Upon learning that they were now citizens of a new country, the people cheered, rang church bells, and pulled down symbols of British rule.

Congress later ordered another copy of the Declaration of Independence to be written out on a heavy paper-like material called **parchment**. A note at the top of this copy said that it was "The unanimous Declaration of the thirteen united States of America." Members of the Second Continental Congress signed this version of the Declaration of Independence on August 2, 1776.

Written on parchment, this version of the Declaration of Independence was signed by 56 delegates. Today, it is one of America's most treasured documents.

IN CONGRESS, July 4, 1776
The unanimous Declaration of the thirteen united States of America

When in the Course of human events, it becomes necessary for one people to dissolve the political bands which have connected them with another, and to assume among the powers of the earth, the separate and equal station to which the Laws of Nature and of Nature's God entitle them, a decent respect to the opinions of mankind requires that they should declare the causes which impel them to the separation.

We hold these truths to be self-evident, that all men are created equal, that they are endowed by their Creator with certain unalienable Rights, that among these are Life, Liberty and the pursuit of Happiness.—That to secure these rights, Governments are instituted among Men, deriving their just powers from the consent of the governed, —That whenever any Form of Government becomes destructive of these ends, it is the Right of the People to alter or to abolish it, and to institute new Government, laying its foundation on such principles and organizing its powers in such form, as to them shall seem most likely to effect their Safety and Happiness. Prudence, indeed, will dictate that Governments long established should not be changed for light and transient causes; and accordingly all experience hath shewn, that mankind are more disposed to suffer, while evils are sufferable, than to right themselves by abolishing the forms to which they are accustomed. But when a long train of abuses and usurpations, pursuing invariably the same Object evinces a design to reduce them under absolute Despotism, it is their right, it is their duty, to throw off such Government, and to provide new Guards for their future security.—Such has been the patient sufferance of these Colonies; and such is now the necessity which constrains them to alter their former Systems of Government. The history of the present King of Great Britain is a history of repeated injuries and usurpations, all having in direct object the establishment of an absolute Tyranny over these States. To prove this, let Facts be submitted to a candid world.

He has refused his Assent to Laws, the most wholesome and necessary for the public good.
He has forbidden his Governors to pass Laws of immediate and pressing importance, unless suspended in their operation till his Assent should be obtained; and when so suspended, he has utterly neglected to attend to them.
He has refused to pass other Laws for the accommodation of large districts of people, unless those people would relinquish the right of Representation in the Legislature, a right inestimable to them and formidable to tyrants only.
He has called together legislative bodies at places unusual, uncomfortable, and distant from the depository of their public Records, for the sole purpose of fatiguing them into compliance with his measures.
He has dissolved Representative Houses repeatedly, for opposing with manly firmness his invasions on the rights of the people.
He has refused for a long time, after such dissolutions, to cause others to be elected; whereby the Legislative powers, incapable of Annihilation, have returned to the People at large for their exercise; the State remaining in the mean time exposed to all the dangers of invasion from without, and convulsions within.
He has endeavoured to prevent the population of these States; for that purpose obstructing the Laws for Naturalization of Foreigners; refusing to pass others to encourage their migrations hither, and raising the conditions of new Appropriations of Lands.
He has obstructed the Administration of Justice, by refusing his Assent to Laws for establishing Judiciary powers.
He has made Judges dependent on his Will alone, for the tenure of their offices, and the amount and payment of their salaries.
He has erected a multitude of New Offices, and sent hither swarms of Officers to harrass our people, and eat out their substance.
He has kept among us, in times of peace, Standing Armies without the Consent of our legislatures.

He has affected to render the Military independent of and superior to the Civil power.

He has combined with others to subject us to a jurisdiction foreign to our constitution, and unacknowledged by our laws; giving his Assent to their Acts of pretended Legislation:

For Quartering large bodies of armed troops among us:

For protecting them, by a mock Trial, from punishment for any Murders which they should commit on the Inhabitants of these States:

For cutting off our Trade with all parts of the world:

For imposing Taxes on us without our Consent:

For depriving us in many cases, of the benefits of Trial by Jury:

For transporting us beyond Seas to be tried for pretended offences

For abolishing the free System of English Laws in a neighbouring Province, establishing therein an Arbitrary government, and enlarging its Boundaries so as to render it at once an example and fit instrument for introducing the same absolute rule into these Colonies:

For taking away our Charters, abolishing our most valuable Laws, and altering fundamentally the Forms of our Governments:

For suspending our own Legislatures, and declaring themselves invested with power to legislate for us in all cases whatsoever.

He has abdicated Government here, by declaring us out of his Protection and waging War against us.

He has plundered our seas, ravaged our Coasts, burnt our towns, and destroyed the lives of our people.

He is at this time transporting large Armies of foreign Mercenaries to complete the works of death, desolation and tyranny, already begun with circumstances of Cruelty & perfidy scarcely paralleled in the most barbarous ages, and totally unworthy the Head of a civilized nation.

He has constrained our fellow Citizens taken Captive on the high Seas to bear Arms against their Country, to become the executioners of their friends and Brethren, or to fall themselves by their Hands.

He has excited domestic insurrections amongst us, and has endeavoured to bring on the inhabitants of our frontiers, the merciless Indian Savages, whose known rule of warfare, is an undistinguished destruction of all ages, sexes and conditions. In every stage of these Oppressions We have Petitioned for Redress in the most humble terms: Our repeated Petitions have been answered only by repeated injury. A Prince whose character is thus marked by every act which may define a Tyrant, is unfit to be the ruler of a free people.

Nor have We been wanting in attentions to our British brethren. We have warned them from time to time of attempts by their legislature to extend an unwarrantable jurisdiction over us. We have reminded them of the circumstances of our emigration and settlement here. We have appealed to their native justice and magnanimity, and we have conjured them by the ties of our common kindred to disavow these usurpations, which, would inevitably interrupt our connections and correspondence. They too have been deaf to the voice of justice and of consanguinity. We must, therefore, acquiesce in the necessity, which denounces our Separation, and hold them, as we hold the rest of mankind, Enemies in War, in Peace Friends.

We, therefore, the Representatives of the united States of America, in General Congress, Assembled, appealing to the Supreme Judge of the world for the rectitude of our intentions, do, in the Name, and by Authority of the good People of these Colonies, solemnly publish and declare, That these United Colonies are, and of Right ought to be Free and Independent States; that they are Absolved from all Allegiance to the British Crown, and that all political connection between them and the State of Great Britain, is and ought to be totally dissolved; and that as Free and Independent States, they have full Power to levy War, conclude Peace, contract Alliances, establish Commerce, and to do all other Acts and Things which Independent States may of right do. And for the support of this Declaration, with a firm reliance on the protection of divine Providence, we mutually pledge to each other our Lives, our Fortunes and our sacred Honor.

The purpose of the Declaration of Independence was to announce that the United States of America was a new country, separate from Britain. But the Congress also wanted to explain why the colonies had decided to declare their freedom.

The Declaration starts by saying that certain truths are "self-evident," or obviously true. One of these truths is that "all men are created equal." These words mean that before governments existed, no one had a right to rule anyone else. Each man was his own ruler and was therefore equal to everyone else. Another truth is that people have "inalienable Rights," which include "Life, Liberty, and the Pursuit of Happiness." All men deserve to live life freely and do what will make them happy. Governments, the Declaration claims, are formed to protect these rights.

By signing the Declaration of Independence, the delegates were betraying Britain. If captured, they would be jailed and most likely put to death.

"*The principles contained in* [the Declaration of Independence] *are saving principles. Stand by those principles, be true to them on all occasions, in all places, against all foes, and at whatever cost.*"

—Frederick Douglass, African American leader and writer, July 5, 1852

The Declaration goes on to say that if a government does not protect its people's rights, the people have the right to change it or replace it. But overturning a government is serious and must be undertaken for serious reasons. Only after a government has committed a "long train of abuses" should citizens consider replacing it. This was the situation the colonists were in, says the Declaration. King George III had trampled on their rights over and over again. Then the Declaration lists all the abuses the colonists suffered at the hands of the king. Such a man, it said, was "unfit to be the ruler of a free people" like the Americans. The Declaration also blamed the British people for not supporting the Americans.

In 1776, Americans were most excited about the last part of the Declaration. Using the words of Lee's resolution, it declared, "these United Colonies are, and of Right ought to be Free and Independent States." Also, "all political connection between them and the State of Great Britain, is and ought

The Declaration of Independence attacked King George III, calling him a tyrant who was not fit to rule the American colonists.

to be totally dissolved." Finally, the Declaration says that because the new states are independent, they have the same political powers as any other country.

An Inspiration

In 1989, protesters crowded Tiananmen Square in the capital city of Beijing, China, to demand more freedom. The Declaration of Independence provided inspiration for many of the demonstrators.

Many people believe the Declaration of Independence is one of the most important political documents ever written. Its powerful ideas of equality and liberty have inspired people throughout the world. Shortly after the American colonists gained independence, for example, the citizens of France rose up against their own king in the French Revolution. In the early 1800s, revolutions moved through Spain, Portugal, Greece, and many South American countries. More recently, in 1989, Chinese citizens protested against their government in the capital city of Beijing. Some demonstrators stood in Beijing's Tiananmen Square and read the Declaration of Independence out loud for inspiration.

The idea of equality stayed with Americans long after the Declaration of Independence was signed. It spoke to women, blacks, and other groups who had not been given the same basic rights as white men. Even today, certain groups continue to struggle for equality in America.

Women worked for rights equal to those of men, including the right to vote. In 1848, a group fighting for women's rights met in Seneca Falls, New York. They used the Declaration of Independence as the model for their own document, the Declaration of Sentiments. In their Declaration, the women proclaimed, "all men and women are created equal."

Women made great steps toward equality when they won the right to vote in 1920.

The Declaration of Independence was also important in the fight against slavery. In the years following the Revolutionary War, many Americans saw that owning someone takes away his or her right to life and liberty. This idea led many northern states to end slavery. The Declaration also swayed President Abraham Lincoln in his decision to free black slaves during the Civil War (1861–1865). But blacks still weren't equal. A century later, they were still fighting for such freedoms as equal education, equal job opportunities, and an equal right to vote. In 1964, the **Civil Rights** Act was passed, giving blacks and all other people equal rights under the law.

Women in Brooklyn, New York, demonstrate for the right to vote.

In his famous 1963 speech, "I Have a Dream," civil rights leader Martin Luther King Jr. talked about the Declaration of Independence. He said, "I have a dream that one day this nation will rise up and live out the true meaning of its creed: 'We hold these truths to be self-evident that all men are created equal.'"

25

The Declaration of Independence has always been an inspiration to immigrants. Its promise of freedom is what brought many people to the United States. The event that is perhaps most symbolic of the Declaration's promise is held each year on the Fourth of July at Monticello, Thomas Jefferson's home in Virginia. Here, in a ceremony each Fourth of July, immigrants become new citizens. Along with other Americans, they celebrate the document that created the United States. And they remember what it stands for—the equality and rights of all people.

On July 4, 2003, a judge swore in 77 new U.S. citizens at Monticello, Thomas Jefferson's home in Virginia. This ceremony is held every year on Independence Day to celebrate America's birthday.

The Second Continental Congress ordered an official copy of the Declaration of Independence be made on parchment. This copy is the one the delegates later signed and kept safe. During the Revolutionary War, the Declaration was rolled up and moved every time British forces neared the delegates' meeting place. The document was kept in the White House after it was built in 1800. When the British attacked Washington, D.C., during the War of 1812 (1812–1815), the Declaration was saved from fire and stored in Leesburg, Virginia. During World War II (1939–1945), it was placed in a secure container at Fort Knox, Kentucky.

The Declaration of Independence was first displayed to the public in 1841. Sunlight and moisture made the parchment crinkle and the ink fade. By the mid-1900s, scientists were searching for the best way to preserve the document. Today, the Declaration is displayed in the Rotunda of the National Archives Building in Washington, D.C. It is stored in an airtight metal container made of titanium and aluminum. Visitors can see the Declaration through special glass that helps protect the document. Experts continue to study new preservation methods. They keep careful watch over the condition of the Declaration of Independence to make sure it will be viewed by generations to come.

In 1952, the Declaration of Independence was put on display in the Rotunda of the National Archives Building in Washington, D.C.

Time Line

June 17, 1775

The Battle of Bunker Hill in Boston

May 10, 1775

The Second Continental Congress meets in Philadelphia.

April 19, 1775

The Battles of Lexington and Concord; the Revolutionary War begins.

1767

Parliament passes the Townshend Acts.

1754-1763

The French and Indian War

May, 1607

English settlers establish Jamestown, Virginia.

1775

1774

Parliament passes the Intolerable Acts.

The First Continental Congress meets in Philadelphia on September 5.

1770

1750

1600

1765

Parliament passes the Stamp Act.

December 16, 1773

The Boston Tea Party

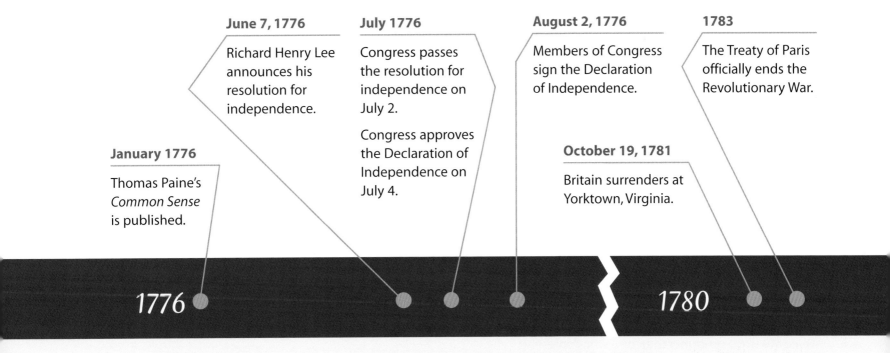

June 7, 1776

Richard Henry Lee announces his resolution for independence.

July 1776

Congress passes the resolution for independence on July 2.

Congress approves the Declaration of Independence on July 4.

August 2, 1776

Members of Congress sign the Declaration of Independence.

1783

The Treaty of Paris officially ends the Revolutionary War.

January 1776

Thomas Paine's *Common Sense* is published.

October 19, 1781

Britain surrenders at Yorktown, Virginia.

1776

1780

The World in Colonial Times

While the American colonies were struggling for independence and starting a new country, what else was happening in the world?

★ Catherine II, known as Catherine the Great, becomes the empress of Russia in 1762.

★ France gives up land in the New World west of the Mississippi River to Spain in 1763.

★ Wolfgang Amadeus Mozart writes his first symphony in 1764.

★ A steam-powered carriage believed to be the first automobile is invented in France by Nicholas Cugnot in 1770.

★ The city of San Francisco, California, is founded in 1776.

★ British explorer Captain James Cook lands his ship in Hawaii in 1778.

★ The waltz becomes a popular dance in 1780.

★ Russia establishes the first permanent settlement in Alaska in 1784.

★ The French Revolution starts on July 14, 1789.

Glossary

ammunition (am-yuh-NISH-uhn) items such as bullets or bombs that can be fired from weapons

boycott (BOI-kaht) to refuse to buy something as a way of protesting

broadside (BRAWD-side) a large sheet of paper usually printed on one side

civil rights (SIV-uhl RITES) the rights that a country's citizens have by law; in the United States, civil rights often mean the rights described in the Constitution, such as freedom of speech and freedom of religion

colonist (KOL-uh-nist) someone who lives in a newly settled area

delegate (DEL-uh-guht) someone who represents other people at a meeting; the delegates to the Continental Congress represented the governments and people of their colonies

export (EK-sport) a product a country sends to be sold in another country

immigrant (IM-uh-gruhnt) someone who travels from one country to live permanently in another country

import (IM-port) a product brought to a country from somewhere else

inherit (in-HAYR-it) to receive money, property, or a title from someone who has died

militia (muh-LISH-uh) a group of citizens who are trained to fight in times of emergency

monarchy (MON-ark-ee) a form of government that has a king or a queen as the ruler

parchment (PARCH-muhnt) a heavy, paperlike material made from the skin of a sheep or goat

parliament (par-luh-muhnt) a group of people elected to make laws for a country

petition (puh-TISH-uhn) a letter signed by many people to someone who is in power, asking for changes in a policy or law

resolution (rez-uh-LOO-shuhn) a formal statement that is voted on by a group

tyranny (TEER-uh-nee) the cruel or unjust rule of people

Fireworks light up the sky on the Fourth of July.

To Learn More

READ THESE BOOKS

Burgan, Michael. *The Declaration of Independence.* Minneapolis: Compass Point Books, 2001.

Fink, Sam. *The Declaration of Independence: The Words that Made America.* New York: Scholastic, 2002.

Fradin, Dennis B. *The Signers: The Fifty-Six Stories Behind the Declaration of Independence.* New York: Walker, 2002.

Freedman, Russell. *Give Me Liberty! The Story of the Declaration of Independence.* New York: Holiday House, 2000.

Hossell, Karen Price. *The Boston Tea Party: Rebellion in the Colonies.* Chicago: Heinemann, 2002.

Rappaport, Doreen. *Victory or Death! Eight Stories of the American Revolution.* New York: HarperCollins, 2003.

Sherrow, Victoria. *Thomas Jefferson.* Minneapolis: Lerner, 2003.

LOOK UP THESE INTERNET SITES

Battlefields of the Revolution
www.nps.gov/thst/battle.htm
View a state-by-state listing of all battlefields of the Revolutionary War, with links to each location.

The History Channel: The Declaration of Independence
www.historychannel.com/exhibits/declaration/main.html
Learn more about the Declaration of Independence and take a quiz to test your knowledge.

Liberty! The American Revolution
www.pbs.org/ktca/liberty
Explore information about the Revolutionary War and life in the American colonies; and play a game that traces the colonists' decision to declare independence.

Monticello—the Home of Thomas Jefferson
www.monticello.org
Learn more about the many talents of Thomas Jefferson and study detailed information about his political career and the home and gardens he designed.

INTERNET SEARCH KEY WORDS

Colonial America, Boston Tea Party, Intolerable Acts, Continental Congress, Thomas Jefferson, Declaration of Independence

Index